P9-CAO-335

# MOUNT ST. HELENS

### NATIONAL VOLCANIC MONUMENT

The Rebirth of
Mount St. Helens

by

BARBARA DECKER

SIERRA PRESS
MARIPOSA, CA

## DEDICATION

For Bob
—B.D.

Author royalties from this book
will be donated to the
Robert W. Decker Memorial Scholarship
at the
Center for The Study of Active Volcanoes
(CSAV)
—an organization he founded—
at the University of Hawaii, Hilo.

## ACKNOWLEDGMENTS

A big thank you to Gregg Pohll and Todd
Cullings at Coldwater Ridge Visitor Center
and Peter Frenzen at Monument Headquarters in Amboy, Washington, for their input,
guidance, and fact checking. Special thanks
to Jim Adams and Sue Kirk of Northwest
Interpretive Association for their encour-
agement and support during the produc-
tion of this publication.    —JDN

**INSIDE FRONT COVER**
Mount St. Helens with growing dome and Mount
Hood, August 2005. PHOTO ©BRUCE ELY/THE OREGONIAN
**PAGE 2**
The eruption of Mount St. Helens, May 18, 1980.
PHOTO ©ROBERT KRIMMEL
**TITLE PAGE**
Before, During, and After: Mount St. Helens seen
from Yale Lake. PHOTO ©STEVE TERRILL
**PAGE 4 (BELOW)**
Mount St. Helens seen from Johnston Ridge.
PHOTO ©DENNIS FLAHERTY
**PAGE 4/5**
Pre-eruption view of Spirit Lake and Mount St.
Helens, sunset. PHOTO ©BOB and IRA SPRING

# CONTENTS

**PAGE 6/7**
Spirit Lake and Mount St. Helens, October 2004.
PHOTO ©TYSON FISHER
**PAGE 7 (BELOW)**
Douglas-fir seedling on the Pumice Plain.
PHOTO ©ROGER WERTH

7

# MOUNT ST. HELENS

Aerial view Mounts Hood, St. Helens, and Jefferson, June 2005. USGS PHOTO by JOHN PALLISTER

Just before our plane was due to land in Portland, Oregon on May 19, the pilot came on the intercom and announced to us, "I'm going to fly just a little farther north so that you can have a look at something you've never seen before." He was right, and it was a sight we could hardly believe. As the plane banked and slowly circled we could see the angry, shattered stump of Mount St. Helens, with fumes still rising from its gaping crater.

When we had flown out of Portland just a few days earlier, we had marveled at the clear view of the beautiful, symmetrical, snow-covered mountain, 9,677 feet high, with a tiny crater in its summit. The broken mountain we saw now was 8,364 feet high, with a huge, jagged crater that was tilted toward the north, where the forest was blown down for as far as we could see.

The first crater on the summit of Mount St. Helens, March 27, 1980. USGS PHOTO by DAVID FRANK

I was traveling with five geologists from the Hawaiian Volcano Observatory (HVO), including my husband Bob, who was the Scientist-In-Charge there. We had all spent time at Mount St. Helens in April and early May, when the volcano was just stirring to life, but we had gone back to work in Hawaii when it seemed that the early volcanic activity could continue for quite a while. We all lived in Hawaii Volcanoes National Park—our houses were on the rim of Kilauea Crater, and we were all familiar with eruptions there. But Hawaiian eruptions are different: instead of the sudden explosive ferocity of stratovolcanoes like Mount St. Helens, Hawaii's volcanoes erupt more "quietly," with high fountains of incandescent lava and long fluid lava flows that can travel for many miles. The eruptions are spectacular, but very rarely deadly. While we had all seen the results of explosive eruptions in other countries, Mount St. Helens had a special immediacy: it was in the United States, and besides, the eruption had taken the life of one of our colleagues.

Phreatic eruption, Spring, 1980. USGS PHOTO

The first reports of the climactic May 18 eruption took a couple of hours to reach Hawaii. But by that afternoon we were on the plane to San Francisco and then on the first flight to Portland the next morning. We joined the scientists who had come to Vancouver, Washington, from all over the country—and soon those from all over the world—to study the most destructive volcanic eruption in the history of the United States.

Ironically, the day before—at just about the same time on the morning of May 18—two geologists, Keith and Dorothy Stoffel, were in a light plane circling around Mount St. Helens just as a magnitude 5.1 earthquake shook the mountain. They saw several small rockfalls start down the steeply sloping crater walls, and seconds later

Eruption plume, May 18, 1980.
USGS PHOTO by DONALD A. SWANSON

*A hurricane of hot rock, ash, and gas bursts outward. Note landslide at lower right corner. PHOTO ©KEITH RONNHOLM

*The expanding blast cloud, May 18, 1980.
PHOTO ©KEITH RONNHOLM

*The blast cloud rolls across the landscape, May 18, 1980.
PHOTO ©KEITH RONNHOLM

were the closest witnesses to the onset of the largest landslide in recorded history, closely followed by a huge volcanic eruption. "The whole north side of the summit crater began to move instantaneously as one gigantic mass. The nature of movement was eerie, not like anything we'd ever seen before," Dorothy recalled. "The entire mass began to ripple and churn without moving laterally. Then the whole north side of the summit started moving to the north along a deep-seated plane."

Seconds later, a massive explosion shook the mountain. An explosion cloud mushroomed sideways to the north and plunged down the slope, but in the plane they neither felt nor heard the explosion. Realizing the enormous size of the eruption, they dived at full throttle to gain speed, but the expanding cloud seemed to be gaining on them. By turning south, away from the direction of the blast, they finally outdistanced it. Behind them, rapidly growing ash clouds thrust north and northwest. To the east, the black clouds rose into billowing mushroom shapes and lightning bolts, thousands of meters high, shot through them. Half an hour later, the Stoffels, shaken but safe, landed at the Portland airport.

In the first weeks after the catastrophic eruption the scientific focus, especially for those of us from HVO, was on documenting what had happened—and what the volcano might do next. It was a chance to study geology in real time. But soon scientists and researchers of many disciplines from all over the world started arriving to conduct experiments—some of which would last for many years. Nature doesn't often provide a virtually clean slate for scientists to study how life—in its many forms—returns to a landscape that has been so devastatingly altered.

In the years since 1980, volcanologists have made great strides in refining their understanding of how volcanoes work, and in developing new techniques and instruments for monitoring that are now used on dangerous volcanoes all over the world. Biologists, botanists, plant ecologists, and other scientists have made many important discoveries. The amazingly complex interactions among surviving plants and animals—and the "colonizers" that arrived from the outside—have contradicted long-held ecological theories and opened doors to exciting new research.

A mathematician friend of ours once remarked to us that he could never stand to be a geologist. When we asked him why, he replied, "Because the answers keep changing." For us, the most exciting and rewarding aspect of the past quarter-century of research at Mount St. Helens has been seeing how many of the answers have kept changing—evolving would be a better word—bringing new understanding in surprising ways to many fields of science.

*Ninety seconds after the eruption the blast cloud approaches Bear Meadow, 11.5 miles from the mountain.
PHOTO ©KEITH RONNHOLM

*This extraordinary sequence of the eruption of Mount St. Helens was made by Keith Ronnholm from what he believed was a safe distance at Bear Meadow, 11.5 miles from the mountain. It required only 90 seconds for the blast to reach his location—a speed of more than 450 m.p.h.! The image on page 11 was made after he retreated from Bear Meadow

**ABOVE:** *The enormous eruption plume rises above the shattered forest, May 18, 1980. PHOTO ©KEITH RONNHOLM

**PAGE 12/13:** Mount St. Helens and North Fork of the Toutle River from Castle Lake Viewpoint, sunset. PHOTO ©TYSON FISHER

**ABOVE:** The lush forest of the Mount St. Helens area as it existed prior to the eruption. PHOTO ©JEFF D. NICHOLAS

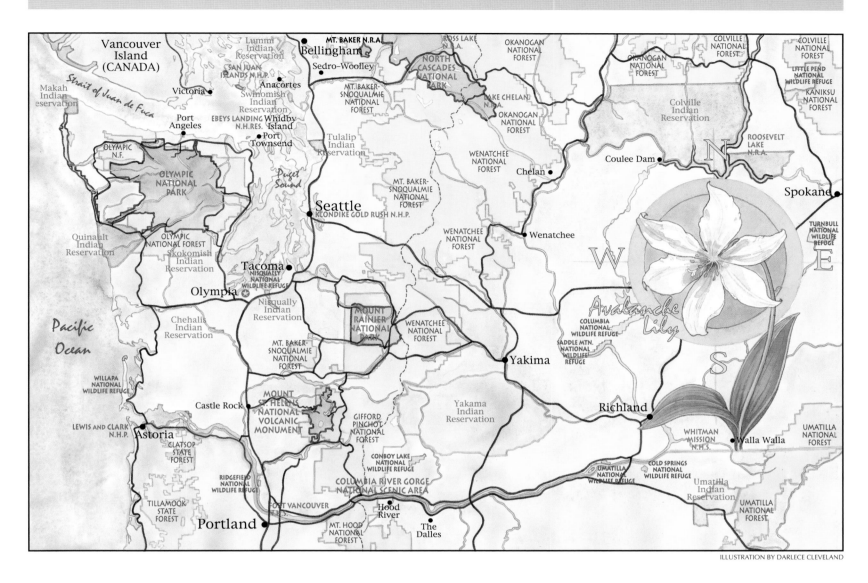

ILLUSTRATION BY DARLECE CLEVELAND

The vast region considered as the Pacific Northwest is bounded on the west by the Pacific Ocean, on the south by California and Nevada, on the north by Canada, and on the east by the Rocky Mountains. It is an area of almost unbelievable beauty and diversity. Fortunate Northwesterners live within reach of uncrowded ocean beaches, untamed rivers, mountain wilderness, dense forests, and open rangeland.

At the heart of all this munificence is the beautiful Cascade Range of mountains, stretching from southern British Columbia to south of the California border. On a clear day in the Northwest it is hard to be out of sight of a volcano. Moisture-laden storm clouds moving in from the Pacific Ocean drop most of their precipitation on the west side of this great mountain range, so the western slopes are cloaked in dense, mossy forests—mostly of Douglas-fir.

On the eastern, drier side of the mountains are rolling foothills with more open forests, principally ponderosa pine, giving way to open grassy range and farmlands.

But the Cascades are not ordinary mountains: they are a chain of tall, ice-covered volcanoes, some of which have been active in historic time. Just this northwest portion of the Cascade Range contains five volcanic national parks and monuments: from the ancient volcanic rocks in North Cascades National Park Service Complex, south to glacier-clad Mount Rainier National Park, and restless Mount St. Helens National Volcanic Monument in Washington, and Newberry Crater National Volcanic Monument and Crater Lake National Park in Oregon, where an improbably blue lake fills the crater of a shattered volcano.

Before the major eruption of Mount St. Helens in 1980, many people in the Northwest were unaware—or had forgotten—that these were living mountains, capable of stirring to action at any time. But the early Indians of the Northwest recognized their danger, making up legends about the mountains that have been handed down for generations. Tribal legends vary somewhat, but for one tribe Mount St. Helens is seen as an ugly witch, who over time can change into a beautiful maiden. Unfortunately, the transformation works the other way too; over the past four thousand years of periodic volcanic activity, Mount St. Helens has transformed from burning witch to sleeping beauty and back again several times. We are lucky enough to see the beginning of the next cycle of natural renewal and glimpse the tranquil beauty of Mount St. Helens' future.

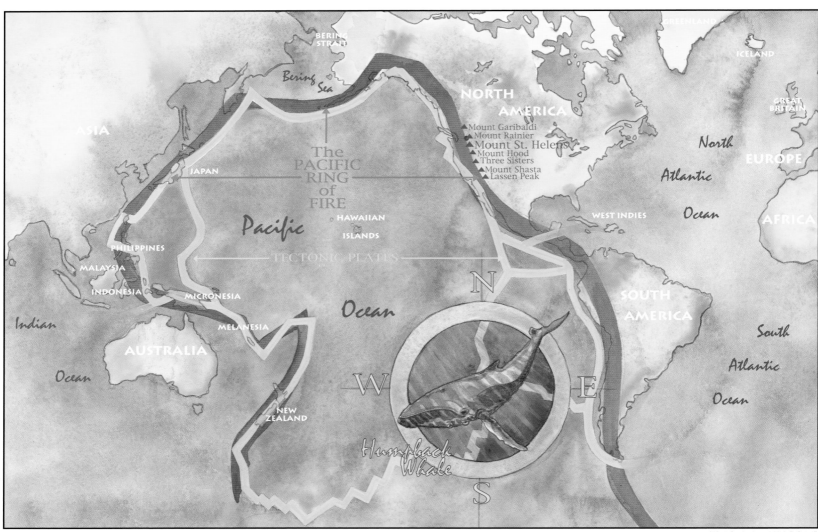

ILLUSTRATION BY DARLECE CLEVELAND

Most of the world's volcanoes occur in belts or chains, like great beads on a giant string. Sometimes the chains are quite straight, but more often they form gently curving arcs. The "Ring of Fire" around the Pacific Ocean is a series of great arcs of volcanoes, that together form a nearly complete circle around the water hemisphere of the Earth.

One segment of the Ring of Fire extends for one thousand kilometers, from northern California's Lassen Peak in the south, with dozens of volcanic peaks and smaller volcanic features, to British Columbia's Mount Garibaldi in the north. These are the volcanoes of the spectacular Cascade Range, and Mount St. Helens is one of them.

In addition to the circum-Pacific ring of volcanoes, another major volcanic belt extends from the Mediterranean Sea through Iran and, after a gap, continues through Indonesia to the Pacific belt. Indonesia has one hundred twenty seven live volcanoes, second only to the United States as the country on Earth with the largest number of potentially active volcanoes.

The Ring of Fire and the Mediterranean–Indonesian belt together account for 80 percent of the world's known volcanoes on land. However, a conventional world map tells only part of the story: what it does not reveal is that most of the world's volcanoes are hidden beneath the ocean. Maps of the terrain under the sea show great mid-ocean ridges that are apparently capped by hundreds of live volcanoes.

For many years geologists and geographers puzzled as to why most volcanoes occur in linear or arcuate chains rather than at random points on the earth's surface; now the concept of plate tectonics offers an answer to this question. The idea that segments of the earth's crust are slowly moving over large horizontal distances—thousands of kilometers—was first seriously proposed in the early 1900s by an Austrian scientist named Alfred Wegener. He called his innovative concept "continental drift" and envisioned great rafts of rigid continental crust slowly and majestically drifting through a highly viscous oceanic crust, a controversial idea that most scientists of his day would not accept.

Wegener's idea was given new life

and a new twist in the 1960s, when oceanographers and geophysicists made a breakthrough discovery that the seafloor crust is made up of belts of rocks that are magnetized in long, linear patterns, parallel to the mid-ocean ridges and symmetrical on both sides of the ridges. These patterns indicated that new seafloor is being created at the mid-ocean ridges, and slowly spreading away from the rifts in opposite directions. They were shown to be moving at speeds of one to ten centimeters per year, about the rate at which fingernails grow. The oceanographers called this process "seafloor spreading," and the geophysicists called it "plate tectonics."

According to the plate tectonics concept, the earth's surface is broken into a dozen major plates, fifty to one hundred kilometers thick, which move about horizontally with respect to one another. These plates "float" and "slide" on a highly viscous layer in the earth's mantle beneath them. In comparison to the earth's diameter, the plates are comparable to broken pieces of shell on a soft-boiled egg. This concept differs from Wegener's idea mainly in that many of the plates are made up of both continental and oceanic crust, with the continents riding passively on the spreading seafloor like ships locked into a drifting ice floe.

The main action in plate tectonics occurs at the edges of the plates—earthquakes and volcanic eruptions on human timescales; splitting, shifting, and crumpling continents on geologic timescales. Between the separating plates is a zone of "healed" cracks, such as the Mid-Atlantic Ridge. The converging plates override one another by thrusting and folding rocks into great mountain ranges like the Himalayas, and side-slipping plates create notorious fault zones like the San Andreas in California, the Alpine in New Zealand, and the Anatolia in Turkey.

Where tectonic plates are moving apart, volcanoes fill the separating scars of the diverging plates with lava flows. They create new seafloor along the crests of mid-ocean ridges and are known as rift volcanoes. Volcanoes also build high peaks along the crumpled zones where the plates are slowly colliding. In this situation, the volcanoes do not form at the exact contact of the plates; that zone is generally a deep oceanic trench. Plates converge by one overriding the other, usually an oceanic edge plunging or subducting beneath a continental edge. The portions of plates covered by deep oceans are more dense and thinner than the parts of plates that carry continental land masses.

Subduction-related volcanoes occur about two hundred kilometers inland from the oceanic trench. The reason they are so far inland from the plate margin is not clear, but it is probably related to a zone of extensive vertical fractures caused by the buckling of the overlying plate. Also, these volcanoes are located atop the general area where the subducting plate has reached a depth of about 100 kilometers; the high temperatures within the earth at this depth and the lowered melting temperatures of the rocks (caused by the addition of water and carbon dioxide from seafloor sediments that are dragged down on the subducting plate) seem to make the Pacific Northwest an ideal region for the formation of large batches of magma.

The Ring of Fire volcanoes around the rim of the Pacific Ocean, and the Mediterranean–Indonesian volcanic belt, all belong to the subduction volcano class. Because the subducting plates generally push beneath the overriding plates at angles of thirty to sixty degrees, these contact zones trace arcs on the sphere of the Earth. The island arcs of New Zealand, the southwest Pacific, Indonesia, the Philippines, Japan, Kuriles, Kamchatka, the Aleutians, and the Caribbean are famous for their subduction volcanoes. The western spine of North and South America—the Cascade Range, the highlands of Mexico and Central America, and the Andes Range—complete the eastern side of the Ring of Fire.

About one thousand active subduction volcanoes occur along the edges of converging plates and, in any one year, about forty of these will be in some state of eruption. A few, such as Stromboli in Italy, have been erupting almost continuously for centuries. Others, such as Mount Pinatubo in the Philippines, have erupted only once in recorded history. In general, the longer the period between eruptions, the greater the likelihood that the next eruption will be a big one. It is clear from location alone that volcanic activity and plate tectonics are closely related; the edges of the tectonic plates account for more than 95 percent of the world's active volcanoes.

Mount St. Helens and the other volcanoes of the Cascade Range are located on the subduction zone between the small Juan de Fuca Plate and the North America Plate. The most recognizable peaks include Mount Garibaldi in British Columbia; Mount Baker, Glacier Peak, and Mount Adams in Washington; Mount Hood, Mount Jefferson, the Three Sisters, Mount Thielsen, Crater Lake (Mount Mazama), and Mount McLoughlin in Oregon; and Mount Shasta and Lassen Peak in California. In addition, the region includes many cinder cones, lava flows, and other evidence of volcanism.

While the volcanoes of Alaska and Hawaii erupt relatively often, the only two volcanoes in the contiguous United States to erupt in the twentieth century were in the Cascade Range—Mount St. Helens and Lassen Peak. In the eighteenth and nineteenth centuries, though, there are historical records of eruptions of Mount Baker, Glacier Peak, and Mount Rainier, as well as Oregon's Mount Hood and probably Mount Shasta in California. Could the Cascade Range again enter a period of restless activity? The answer is yes, of course—these volcanoes are still young enough to have the unpredictability of youth.

The human history of the Mount St. Helens region of the Pacific Northwest began at least 7,000 years ago with groups of Native Americans living in the area. The Cowlitz and the Klikitat were the principal tribes but others, such as the Salish and the Nisqually, also moved through the countryside. Most spent the wet winters in the lowlands, but moved higher into the mountains as the weather warmed, berries ripened, and game was more plentiful. Their legends show that they recognized Mount St. Helens and the neighboring volcanoes as living mountains and they regarded them with respect and reverence.

The first recorded sighting of Mount St. Helens by a European was by famed British explorer George Vancouver when he sailed his ship up the Northwest coast in 1792, looking for the elusive Northwest Passage. As they passed the mouth of the Columbia River in October of that year, he saw the beautiful snowy peak and named it after his British mentor, Lord Fitzherbert, Baron of St. Helens.

The next mention of a sighting of the volcano appears in the journals of explorers Lewis and Clark, as they traveled down the Columbia in 1805. In his journal, William Clark called Mount St. Helens "The most noble looking object of its kind in nature." None of these early explorers saw Mount St. Helens in eruption, but word-of-mouth reports from local Indians living in the area indicate that it probably erupted several times around 1800.

Trappers and fur traders moved into the Northwest in the early-nineteenth century. When the potential wealth of the plentiful furs became known, the British-owned North West Fur Company established outposts and forts throughout the area. That company eventually became the Hudson's Bay Company, headquartered at Fort Vancouver, near the base of Mount St. Helens in what is now the city of Vancouver, Washington.

By the mid-nineteenth century settlers and missionaries were traveling the Oregon Trail to the Columbia Basin. In 1836, a Dr. Gardner of Fort Vancouver gave the first eyewitness account of a Mount St. Helens eruption. Other settlers reported eruptions during the 1840s and 1850s, with the greatest activity in 1842. A bill designating the Oregon Territory was passed in 1848, and, in 1853, President Fillmore signed another bill that separately designated the Washington Territory.

Southwestern Washington really began to open up to settlement in the 1870s, when the Northern Pacific Railroad arrived. Besides bringing many homesteaders, the railroad opened the region's natural resources to mining and timber interests.

Mining exploration began as early as 1892, and soon after 1900 hundreds of mining claims had been filed. Prospectors were looking chiefly for copper, gold, and silver. The mines were never profitable, though, and most mining activity had ended by 1930.

The timber industry was another story. The rich native forests of huge old-growth trees were irresistible to logging companies, who pushed farther and farther up the river valleys toward Mount St. Helens. At the same time, the population of the region was growing dramatically and Mount St. Helens—especially beautiful blue Spirit Lake—became an increasingly popular destination for recreation. Organizations like the YMCA and Boy Scouts of America built popular summer camps on the lake's shore. After the road up the Toutle River to Spirit Lake was paved in the mid-1940s, recreational use increased. Several rustic resorts were built and many private cabins ringed the lake on U.S. Forest Service land.

The combination of pressures from tourism and from logging interests was an uneasy one. Even as recreational use of the area was increasing every year, the logging companies were pushing closer to Gifford Pinchot National Forest and trying to get concessions to log some of the federal lands. Mount St. Helens made the question irrelevant on May 18, 1980. Every trace of development at Spirit Lake was destroyed and so were 230 square miles of mature, old-growth forest.

**ABOVE:** Paul Kane's painting of Native Americans viewing an eruption of Mount St. Helens, circa 1845. WITH PERMISSION OF THE ROYAL ONTARIO MUSEUM ©ROM

**ABOVE:** The dome glowing at sunset, seen from Johnston Ridge Observatory.
PHOTO ©BRUCE ELY and STEVEN NEHL/THE OREGONIAN

**PAGE 20/21:** Aerial view of Mount St. Helens, Spirit Lake, and Mount Rainier, May 2005.
PHOTO ©BRUCE ELY/THE OREGONIAN

Mount St. Helens and Mount Adams (left) as seen on April 10, 1980. USGS PHOTO by DONALD A. SWANSON

# THE DAY OF FURY

The sharp earthquake that shook Mount St. Helens on the morning of May 18, 1980 was not especially large as earthquakes go, but it was the trigger for a series of catastrophic events that added up to the largest Cascade Range eruption in historic time.

The earthquake struck at 8:32 in the morning; it was measured at 5.1 on the Richter scale, and was centered about a mile beneath the volcano. For weeks, the north flank of the mountain had been becoming more and more unstable by a huge bulge that was growing above a large intrusion of magma. Shaken loose, the mountainside suddenly started to slide away in a massive avalanche. Even as the avalanche reduced the pressure in the volcano, superheated groundwater flashed to steam and dissolved gases exploding in the magma chamber combined to produce a huge lateral blast that was directed to the north and northwest.

Debris-choked Spirit Lake and Mount Rainier, October 1980.
USGS PHOTO by LYN TOPINKA

The dense, debris-filled steam cloud of the blast surged northward from the broken mountain at speeds of more than 300 miles per hour, devastating everything in their path. The thick black clouds rolled up and over four major ridges and valleys, traveling as far as seventeen miles and devastating an area of about 230 square miles.

Monument scientists have divided the blast effects into three "zones"—depending on the degree of destruction. For the first 7.5 miles, destruction was complete: large old-growth trees were uprooted and swept away. This zone is referred to as the "Tree Removal Zone." Extending as far as 15.5 miles from the crater, in the "Blowdown Zone," all the huge conifer trees—some more than one hundred feet tall—were snapped off and flattened to the ground. In a narrow zone beyond 15.5 miles, the "Scorch Zone," most of the trees were left standing, but were singed or scorched beyond recovery.

Blown down forest above North Fork of the Toutle River.
USGS PHOTO by LYN TOPINKA

Meanwhile, the avalanche was wreaking its own brand of destruction. The gigantic mass of crushed rock and glacial ice roared down into Spirit Lake and into the North Fork of the Toutle River. Exploding steam helped fluidize the surging mass that move as fast as 150 miles per hour. One lobe of the avalanche plunged into the west arm of Spirit Lake. The momentum sent another lobe over a 2,000-foot high ridge adjacent to Spirit Lake and into the South Coldwater Valley, but most funneled down the Toutle River for as far as thirteen miles, leaving huge hummocky deposits between150 and 620 feet thick.

Above the shattered volcano, a vertical explosion of ash and steam began to rise. The heavy ash column initially exploded to an altitude of fifteen miles. Fluctuating somewhat in height, and expanding into a mushroom shape, the eruption would

Mudline and debris, Muddy River, October 1980.
Note USGS scientist in circle. USGS PHOTO by LYN TOPINKA

**OPPOSITE:** The eruption: May 18, 1980. PHOTO ©STEVE TERRILL

Helicopter on the Pumice Plain, September 1980.
USGS PHOTO by TOM CASADEVALL

continue for nine hours. The ash cloud moved to the east at about sixty miles per hour, darkening the sky over half of the state of Washington. Yakima—ninety miles away—was blanketed with four to five inches of ash. Measurable ash fell as far away as central Montana. A day later, Denver also received a light dusting of ash. Within two weeks a cloud of finer ash had circled the globe.

As the eruption cloud mushroomed upward, pyroclastic flows poured from the newly formed crater and started to course down the slopes of Mount St. Helens. Sometimes called by the French name *nuee ardentes* or "glowing clouds", these mixtures of volcanic fragments and gases are extremely hot and race downslope at speeds as high as fifty to eighty miles per hour. These flows covered some of the avalanche deposits, and where they overran parts of Spirit Lake, they generated more explosive steam blasts as they encountered the lakewater.

Mudflow on the Toutle River and Interstate 5 bridge, July 1980. USGS PHOTO by LYN TOPINKA

Mudflows that affected all of the river systems draining Mount St. Helens were another major result of the eruption. These mudflows, often labeled with the Indonesian term *"lahars,"* were composed of a slurry of fine rock particles and volcanic ash mixed with large amounts of water from melting snow and ice—and had the consistency of wet cement. The mudflows on the south and east sides streamed down Pine Creek, Muddy River, Smith Creek, and the South Fork of the Toutle River, scouring stream valleys and destroying some bridges and roads, but the damage was far worse on the north and west sides of Mount St. Helens.

The mudflow that poured down the North Fork of the Toutle River started several hours later and was immense. The water-saturated parts of the debris avalanche started to flow, contributing to the water from melting snow and glacier ice. The flows picked up more loose debris, and overran a Weyerhauser logging camp. Moving at speeds of up to twenty-five miles per hour, the mudflows poured down the rivers picking up trees, boulders, and even houses, destroying everything in their path. Eight bridges on the Toutle River were swept away and as many as 200 homes and cabins were destroyed, as well as thirty-seven miles of the Spirit Lake Highway. Far downstream, mudflow deposits—up to nearly forty feet thick—clogged the channels of the Cowlitz and Columbia Rivers, disrupting ship traffic for weeks.

All this happened in just one day. Thirteen hundred feet of the summit of Mount St. Helens had vanished, leaving a crater more than a mile wide and nearly two miles long. The debris avalanche was more than two-thirds of a cubic mile in volume—enough to cover the city of Seattle to a depth of forty feet—and had set a record as the largest avalanche ever seen.

But nature is resilient; the environment can survive and recover, and the infrastructure can be rebuilt. Not so the fifty-seven lives that were lost in the eruption and its aftermath. They were in different areas and for different reasons—a newspaper photographer, a miner, curious volcano watchers, an innkeeper, loggers, and our friend, geologist David Johnston, whose observation post nearly five miles from the volcano was obliterated by the dense black cloud that engulfed his ridge.

Mudline on trees, Toutle River, July 1980.
USGS PHOTO by LYN TOPINKA

Blowdown below Elk Rock, August 1980.
USGS PHOTO by LYN TOPINKA

Destroyed bridge on Toutle River, May 19, 1980.
PHOTO ©JOHN MARSHALL

Garage buried by mudflow, July 1980.
USGS PHOTO by LYN TOPINKA

Blowdown along Smith Creek, September 1980.
USGS PHOTO by LYN TOPINKA

Logging camp destroyed by South Fork Toutle River
mudflow, May 18, 1980. USGS PHOTO by PHIL CARPENTER

Home inundated by mudflow, July 1980.
USGS PHOTO by LYN TOPINKA

Blowdown around Fawn Lake. Note researchers in boat.
USGS PHOTO by LYN TOPINKA

Bridge destroyed by mudflow, North Fork Toutle River,
May 18, 1980. PHOTO ©ROGER WERTH

Journalist Reid Blackburn's car, May 31, 1980.
USGS PHOTO by DAN DZURISIN

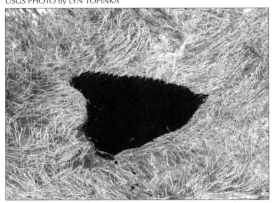

Swirling pattern of the blowdown around Ryan Lake.
PHOTO ©ROGER WERTH

Colorful ponds on the avalanche deposit, August 1980.
USGS PHOTO by LYN TOPINKA

Ashfall along highway near Connell, WA, June 1980.
USGS PHOTO by LYN TOPINKA

**ABOVE:** Debris-choked Spirit Lake following the eruption, May 1980. PHOTO ©ROGER WERTH

David Johnston at Coldwater II Observation Site on May 17, 1980, the day before the eruption.

USGS PHOTO by HARRY GLICKEN

# DAVID A. JOHNSTON

David Johnston was one of fifty-seven people who lost their lives in the May 18, 1980 eruption of Mount St. Helens. Dave was an exceptionally dedicated volcanologist, who worked with just the right combination of curiosity, inventiveness, meticulous observation, and careful interpretation.

His special interest in volcanology was gas geochemistry: monitoring the gases emitted by a volcano to test whether changes in their chemistry might signal an impending eruption. That morning he was also taking measurements of the ominous bulge that was growing rapidly—at a rate averaging five feet per day—on the side of the volcano that loomed across the valley from the observation site.

The location—called Coldwater II Observation Site—had been chosen by geologists for several reasons. The visibility from the ridge was ideal: all the timber had been logged so there were unobstructed views of the mountain, and an old logging road reached this high ridge. It was nearly five miles from the volcano across a deep valley and was considered reasonably safe since almost every recorded volcanic eruption had gone straight up. This case would prove to be the exception; Coldwater II was in the direct path of the lateral blast that engulfed and obliterated the station.

For several weeks, Coldwater II had been manned by a succession of geologists. My husband and another geologist had spent a night there exactly one week earlier. Dave's one night of duty was just on the wrong night.

Dave knew well the hazards of working on active volcanoes. He had worked extensively in Alaska, especially on restless Augustine Volcano. Dave grew up in the distinctly nonvolcanic state of Illinois but was drawn to geology and to volcanology in particular. He graduated from the University of Illinois in 1971, and earned his PhD from the University of Washington in Seattle. In 1978, he joined the U.S. Geological Survey, where his assignment was to monitor volcanic gases in Alaska and the Cascade Range. Dave was one of the first volcanologists on the scene when Mount St. Helens showed signs of reawakening; he worked tirelessly—and with unfailing good humor—until his life was cut short by the great eruption.

Dave was respected as a scientist by his colleagues and valued as a friend by all of us who knew him. In his honor, two major observatories bear his name: the David A. Johnston Cascades Volcano Observatory in Vancouver, Washington, and the Johnston Ridge Observatory in Mount St. Helens National Volcanic Monument.

When the enormity of the May 18th eruption became known, reporters from all over the world converged on Vancouver. Most had covered natural disasters such as floods, hurricanes, and earthquakes, but a volcanic eruption was new to many of them and the terminology was unfamiliar. Weary geologists returning from the field after an eighteen-hour day didn't have time to stop and answer elementary questions, so my husband Bob Decker, who had taught Geology and Volcanology at Dartmouth College, corralled the interested reporters and gave them a quick course in Volcanoes 101, with definitions of the unfamiliar terms:

*Magma* is gas-rich molten rock that is underground; when it reaches the surface it is called *lava*. A *phreatic eruption* is a violent steam explosion with mostly solid fragments of old rock. *Pyroclastic* (literally "fire fragments") means volcanic rock that has been broken into fragments of several sizes: *ash,* which is gritty and nearly the size

of rice; *cinders* which are about the size of golf balls; and *blocks* which are large chunks up to the size of a house. A *volcanic bomb* is a block-sized clot of liquid lava thrown from an erupting volcano, spinning in flight into a rounded shape. The general term for all airfall pyroclastic material from a volcano is *tephra.*

A *pyroclastic flow* (one of the deadliest of volcanic phenomena) is a fluidized mass of hot rock fragments mixed with gases that moves downhill at high speed, while a *lava flow* is a stream of molten rock flowing from a vent. An *ash flow* is a pyroclastic flow of mainly fine-grained, ash-sized particles, and a *mudflow*, or *lahar*, is a water-saturated mass of rock debris that moves rapidly downslope as a liquid. An *ash cloud* is a cloud from an explosive eruption, containing large quantities of volcanic ash—a major hazard to aviation. An *ashfall deposit* consists of pyroclastic fragments that have fallen from an ash cloud.

A *lateral blast* (or *directed blast*)—as hap-

pened at Mount St. Helens—is a volcanic explosion from the side of the mountain instead of the usual vertical blast. A mixture of hot, low-density rock debris, ash, and gas, it moves at high speed over the ground surface.

A *stratovolcano*—such as Mount St. Helens—is a steep volcanic cone built by both lava flows and pyroclastic material; its eruptions are often explosive. A *shield volcano*—such as those in Hawaii—is gently rounded in shape and composed mostly of a sequence of fluid lava flows; its eruptions are usually *effusive.* A *lava dome*—such as the one growing in Mount St. Helens' crater—is a steep-sided, rounded extrusion of lava pushed up from a vent.

An *active volcano* is one that has erupted during historic time. A *dormant volcano* is one that is classified as active but is currently sleeping, with the periods between eruptions called *repose time.* An *extinct volcano* is one that will never erupt again.

**ABOVE:** Phreatic eruptions on the Pumice Plain, Spirit Lake in background, May 18, 1980. PHOTO ©JOHN MARSHALL

**ABOVE:** Pyroclastic flow pouring onto the Pumice Plain, August 7, 1980. USGS PHOTO by PETER W. LIPMAN

# THE ERUPTION

The eruption of Mount St. Helens seen from Yale Lake. PHOTO ©STEVE TERRILL

March 20, 1980. Small earthquakes are not uncommon in volcano country like the Pacific Northwest, but when a quake measuring magnitude 4 on the Richter scale registered that day on the seismographs at the University of Washington in Seattle, seismologists took special notice. It was centered directly below Mount St. Helens and was followed by a swarm of many more small earthquakes. One of the graduate students watching the earthquake signals at the university's seismology lab had previously worked at the Hawaiian Volcano Observatory and recognized a similarity in the earthquake pattern. It resembled the signals recorded in Hawaii when a volcano there is showing signs of the early stages of an eruption. Intrigued, the scientists hurried to install more seismometers on the restless mountain to record and locate the quakes more precisely. The earthquake series continued; during one twelve-hour period in late March the instruments recorded forty-seven earthquakes of magnitude 3 or greater at a shallow depth, directly below Mount St. Helens.

Blowdown and standing singed trees in the backcountry.
PHOTO ©JOHN MARSHALL

On March 27, the first small explosions of steam from the volcano's summit started, forming a crater in the snow-and-ice-covered cone. A few days later, a second small crater opened, sending blue flames into the sky that were visible at night. The next day, there were ninety-three small eruptions of steam and ash, but all the ash was determined to be from old volcanic rock and did not contain any new material. Sometimes these eruptions were single explosions, and at other times there were pulsating jets that lasted for hours. Some columns of steam and ash rose as high as a mile above the summit, and ash falling from the turbulent cloud turned the snow-covered cone gray and black.

Blown down forest near Windy Ridge.
PHOTO ©LARRY ULRICH

On April 1, the seismographs began to record a different kind of earthquake signal known as harmonic tremor, a more continuous ground vibration that is believed to reflect the movement of magma underground. By this time the U.S. Geological Survey (USGS) had sent a team of volcanologists to Mount St. Helens from their other offices in Menlo Park, California; Denver, Colorado; and Hawaii to study the increasing volcanic activity. The idea that an eruption could happen at Mount St. Helens was not entirely unexpected; a report that was published in 1978 turned out to be remarkably prescient.

Since the early 1960s, Dwight Crandell and Donal Mullineaux of the USGS had been conducting a study of the Cascade volcanoes to evaluate the hazards presented by the dormant volcanoes. In their 1978 report they concluded that Mount St. Helens had a dangerous history: it had been more active in the previous 4,500

The blast zone on the north shore of Spirit Lake, May 1980.
PHOTO ©JOHN MARSHALL

**OPPOSITE:** The eruption plume, May 18, 1980. PHOTO ©ROGER WERTH

years than any other volcano in the contiguous United States, with the average interval between eruptive periods of one hundred to one hundred fifty years. In their conclusion they wrote: "In the future Mount St. Helens probably will erupt violently and intermittently just as it has in the recent geologic past, and these future eruptions will affect human life and health, property, agriculture and general economic welfare over a broad area…. The volcano's behavior pattern suggests that the current quiet interval will not last as long as 1,000 years; instead an eruption is more likely to occur within the next 100 years, and perhaps even before the end of this century." Just two years later their forecast came true.

Dwight Crandell and Donal Mullineaux were among the USGS geologists who assembled in Vancouver in April and May of 1980. Researchers in many disciplines from across the country—and soon others from around the world—were arriving to study and try to forecast what Mount St. Helens might do next.

As the earthquakes continued—sometimes as many as fifty per day of magnitude 3 or greater—geologists began to detect another ominous sign: they could see that the mountain's north flank seemed to be distorted. They compared a photo printed in a climbing guide to their view from the same spot and could see that a major deformation was taking place. By the end of April, measurements showed that a huge bulge was moving up and out on the side of the mountain. The bulge was approximately a mile and a half in diameter and had pushed out about 250 feet. By May, the bulge was growing at the rate of five feet per day and had expanded more than four hundred feet to the north—changes that were easily visible to the naked eye.

Eruption history revealed in roadcut. PHOTO JEFF D. NICHOLAS

Scientists concluded that the bulging surface and the earthquake swarm that was directly beneath it were signs that new magma was being injected at a shallow depth below the north flank of Mount St. Helens, and that if this continued a significant eruption was likely. The crucial questions of when it would happen and how large it might be could not be answered.

At the same time, the increasing summit explosions and earthquakes were drawing huge numbers of sightseers to the area, in the hope of seeing something spectacular happen. So many people were flocking to the mountain on highways, logging roads, and trails that Washington governor Dixy Lee Ray made the important but unpopular decision to close the area.

Some exceptions were made. Scientists could still enter the restricted area to continue important research, and private logging companies were allowed to work near the volcano, but were required to equip their workers with sensors to measure the ash content of the air. Unhappy Spirit Lake cabin owners found themselves locked out and protested loudly, but one innkeeper—Harry Truman, owner of Mount St. Helens Lodge—was deputized and allowed to stay. The 83-year-old Truman (always described in news reports as "irascible") found himself a national celebrity—an unlikely hero standing up to the power of Nature. He had lived there for many years and said he was ready for any hand the mountain dealt him.

As days went by, the sheriff complained that people weren't paying attention to the restrictions; eager sightseers were climbing over, or sneaking around, the

Early eruption, April 10, 1980. USGS PHOTO by DONALD A. SWANSON

RED ZONE
HAZARD AREA
ENTRY BEYOND
THIS POINT
BY PERMIT ONLY
ROAD CLOSED
STOP

The "Red Zone", May 17, 1980. PHOTO ©ROGER WERTH

barricades to try to get closer to this once-in-a-lifetime show. It was finally agreed that convoys of cabin owners would be allowed in to collect pets and belongings, but would not be permitted to stay overnight. A convoy went in on May 17, and another group was waiting in line at the barricade on the morning of May 18—expecting to be allowed back in at 10 AM—but at 8:32 Mount St. Helens exploded in a huge eruption.

May 18 and the days that followed changed forever the way the people of the Northwest view their sleeping volcanoes. The statistics were staggering. More than one cubic mile of material had been erupted, leaving a jagged crater 1.8 miles east to west and one-half mile deep, open to the north. The mountain had lost 1,300 feet in altitude. The blast devastated an area of 230 square miles; the avalanche had traveled 13.5 miles and the mudflows 75 miles.

Harry Truman at Spirit Lake Lodge. PHOTO ©ROGER WERTH

The fact that the eruption happened on a Sunday probably saved some lives. Many U.S. Forest Service (USFS) workers had the day off, and most logging operations were shut down for the weekend. One small group of four loggers working sixteen miles to the west, were trapped and badly burned; three later died. Harry Truman's luck ran out that day—he and his lodge were buried by both the huge avalanche and the lateral blast. His memory still lives on at Mount St. Helens: a prominent ridge between Mount Margaret and Johnston Ridge is officially named Harry's Ridge.

Pyroclastic flow debris, May, 1980.
USGS PHOTO by DONALD A. SWANSON

Though the worst of the destruction was over, during the summer and fall of 1980 Mount St. Helens produced smaller explosive episodes five more times, generating ash clouds and pyroclastic flows. Twice between these episodes a lava dome started to grow in the crater. A lava dome is a thick extrusion of viscous lava that pushes up over the vent. Each lava dome grew vigorously, but was blown out by the next explosion.

Geologists studying the volcano hoped to find a way to forecast these eruptive episodes. By careful analysis of the earthquake patterns, and by monitoring the changes in the chemistry of the gas emissions, they were able to successfully forecast several of these events, allowing scientists and USFS employees to evacuate the area safely.

After 1980, most of the eruptions were over except for some small bursts of tephra and gas. A new lava dome in the crater continued to grow episodically, and by the end of 1986 had grown to measure more than 3,500 feet in diameter and loomed more than eight hundred feet above the crater floor.

The dome growing in the crater of Mount St. Helens, April 15, 1983. USGS PHOTO by LYN TOPINKA

By October 1986, the dome growth stopped and Mount St. Helens quieted down. A small glacier—or an "incipient glacier," as experts called it—started to grow between the dome and the crater wall. The work of geologists was just beginning; what they learned and are still learning from Mount St. Helens is helping to revolutionize volcano monitoring and the science of how volcanoes work.

Scientist monitoring early dome, August, 1981.
USGS PHOTO by LYN TOPINKA

Helicopter searching the Pumice Plain following the eruption, May 19, 1980.

PHOTO ©JOHN MARSHALL

# SURVIVORS

At first light on the morning of May 19 searchers were out looking for survivors of the massive eruption. More than a dozen U.S. Army and National Guard helicopters took to the air, flying up and down rivers and roadways looking for people trying to escape. Their efforts were greatly hampered by the ash-filled air and unstable deposits on which to land, besides the ever-present thought that the major eruption might be just pausing before another explosion. In addition, the terrain had been so altered by the avalanche, mudflow, and ash deposits that even pilots who were very familiar with the area could not be sure just where they were. Searchers on foot were out, too, but deposits were so hot—and so many trees were down—that ground travel was almost impossible.

By the end of the first day, 113 people had been rescued; in the next few days the total reached nearly two hundred, the youngest a three-month old baby. None were in the "Red Zone" that had been cordoned off by officials. Some were families out for a camping weekend; some were just curious to see what the mountain was up to. A few were trapped as far away as twenty-five to thirty miles from the volcano; it was unthinkable that destruction could reach that far, until it happened.

Survivors told of harrowing escapes blocked by fallen trees, raging streams, and dense, blinding ash. One couple, camped twenty-four miles from the mountain, described a sea of mud suddenly surging down the river. They climbed on top of their car, but were thrown into the log-filled water and swept downstream until they were rescued from chest-deep mud. Three loggers who were working many miles from the volcano, with the mountain hidden by a ridge, heard a creaking, grinding sound, and then were overwhelmed by the hot blast. Badly burned, they staggered eight miles down the Toutle River in near-darkness before being rescued by helicopter. A local couple treating their young children to their first camping trip found themselves in a nightmare. They took shelter in an abandoned shack while ash and pumice rained down. The next day they tried to hike out, but downed trees blocked their way. Luckily a helicopter pilot spotted them; rescuers on foot then led them to an area where the helicopter could land and carry them to safety. Stories like these still live vividly in the memories of survivors and rescuers, decades later.

**ABOVE:** Eruption plume, July 22, 1980. USGS PHOTO BY MIKE DOUKAS

**PAGE 36/37:** Aerial view of Mount St. Helens' steaming crater, sunset.
PHOTO ©BRUCE ELY/THE OREGONIAN

# THE RECOVERY

Blasted tree stump at Johnston Ridge. PHOTO ©ROGER WERTH

The story of the ongoing ecological recovery from the massive 1980 eruption of Mount St. Helens has been fascinating, especially because of its complexity. It has proven to be an ideal place for scientists to study the intricate interactions that allow ecosystems to respond to large-scale disturbances. Here the "disturbances" came in many forms: the blast zone, the avalanche and mudflow deposits, pyroclastic flows, the blowdown zone, and areas of heavy ashfall. Also, the area affected was an intricate landscape of meadows, forests, lakes, and streams with an immensely diverse population of plants and wildlife. The pace and sequence of recovery has been different in each environment.

John Muir once said, "When we try to pick out something by itself we find it hitched to everything else in the universe." He could have been looking at Mount St. Helens; here the processes of succession and reestablishment are so complex and so intricately intertwined that most textbook models of ecological recovery have proven to be far too simplistic.

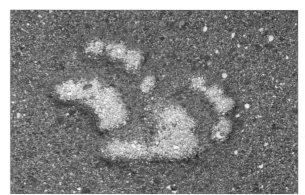

Bear paw prints in ash and pumice, October 1980. USGS PHOTO by LYN TOPINKA

The eruption provided a unique opportunity for hundreds of scientists from different disciplines to conduct ongoing long-term studies into the ecological survival and reestablishment after such a cataclysmic event. The interaction of survivors and colonizers—both plants and animals—has been wonderfully and unexpectedly complex. Monument Scientist Peter Frenzen explains: "The variety of 'experimental' settings created by the volcano have become an important laboratory for testing those ideas…. Animals from the tiniest wood-boring insect to the largest elk appear to be having a profound influence on the developing vegetation. Animals are selecting and colonizing areas on the basis of habitat characteristics and, in turn, helping to shape habitat structure and composition…. Plants representing all major stages of forest development appear to be establishing simultaneously. This contradicts classic ecological theory that describes the orderly establishment and successive replacement of one group of plants by another."

One important factor in the survival and recovery of life around the volcano was the time of year the eruption happened. It was mid-spring, and much of the land at higher elevations was under a blanket of snow. Tiny animals—such as pocket gophers and deer mice—were hibernating in burrows under the snow, just about to emerge. Even the time of day—8:32 in the morning—was important: small nocturnal animals had gone back into their burrows for the day. Even though many did not survive the blast and intense heat, when the survivors emerged—whether from

Lupine flower. PHOTO ©ROGER WERTH

---

**OPPOSITE:** Wildflowers and young seedlings re-populating the area around Windy Ridge, early morning. PHOTO ©CHARLES GURCHE

Seedling near Spirit Lake. PHOTO ©ROGER WERTH

Biologist John Bishop of U of WA studying plant recovery. PHOTO ©ROGER WERTH

Elk herd near The Hummocks. PHOTO ©TYSON FISHER

Fireweed on Harry's Ridge above Spirit Lake, September 1984. USGS PHOTO by LYN TOPINKA

hibernation or from a day's sleep—they brought with them organic soil and fungi where wind blown seeds could take root. One researcher declared the pocket gophers to be the heroes of the recovery process: their mounds of dirt formed oases for blowing seeds to take root. These new plants became the nucleus of a colony of more plants, which in turn attracted returning insects, birds, and animals. As large animals—especially elk and deer—came to browse on the new vegetation, their hooves broke up the hard crust of ash and left footprints where more seeds could collect and grow. The droppings left by the returning animals and birds carried valuable seeds for the emerging "gardens." Even the decomposing bodies of the many animals—large and small—that were killed in the eruption, as well as insects and organic material blown in by the winds, contributed to the development of new soil. The snowbanks had also sheltered a variety of plants and small trees that survived as islands of living foliage when the snow melted.

If the pocket gopher was the hero among animal survivors, the lupine could be considered the heroine of the plant colonizers. On the Pumice Plain, where the land had been covered by avalanche debris, hot mudflows, and, finally, hot pyroclastic flow deposits to a total depth of nearly three hundred feet, scientists looking for the first sign of a colonizing plant finally found a single lupine plant in 1983. Recognizing that lupine had special characteristics that would help it to survive, namely the ability to extract nitrogen from the atmosphere and fix it in the soil, one of the scientists established a taped-off research plot around the plant. He revisited it often to document how the single plant had spread and made a hospitable environment for other plants and insects. He carefully counted the lupine plants over the years; the numbers exceeded 150,000 plants after ten years, overflowing the plot and spilling across the plain. By 2005, the areas that had been nearly devoid of life were carpeted with lupine, grasses, and other herbaceous plants, including small shrubs and a few tree saplings.

The dense old-growth forests around the mountain had consisted of Douglas-fir, western red cedar, noble fir, silver fir, and hemlock, mixed with some deciduous trees like maples, alder, and cottonwood. Almost all were destroyed, shattered, or blown away. Recovery of the forests at Mount St. Helens is taking place in two distinctly different ways. On lands outside the monument boundaries, the U.S. Forest Service and private timber companies immediately began to reforest their lands by clearing the downed trees and replanting millions of seedlings. Some of the young trees have grown so fast that the first stands were thinned and harvested for timber in 2005. Inside the monument, scientists study Nature's method for the healing and recovery of a destroyed forest; a slow, complicated process, but one that should result in a rich combination of conifers, deciduous trees, shrubs, ferns, and mosses instead of the single variety of trees seen in the replanted stands. It is estimated that a healthy young conifer forest could be growing in fifty years—an old-growth forest in 450 years.

The effects of the eruption were devastating on wildlife in the area as well. An estimated 1,500 Roosevelt elk and as many as 5,000 deer were killed that morning, as well as hundreds of bears, coyotes, bobcats, rabbits, and countless birds and insects. But most species turned out to be remarkably tenacious. In the first days after the eruption, insects and birds were flying into the devastated area, and scientists found footprints of animals on ground that had barely started to cool. Researchers studying the wildlife population feared that it would take decades for significant numbers of animals to return, but after only five years the numbers of elk and deer were back to normal and others were almost as successful.

Rainbow trout at Spirit Lake, 2005. PHOTO ©ROGER WERTH

The recovery of the mountain lakes around Mount St. Helens has been another unexpected success story. A lake's exact location made a difference in the degree of damage it suffered; a covering of snow and ice gave some protection, but most were inundated with rocks, trees, debris, hot ash, and dead animals, which completely altered the waters' chemistry.

The effects on Spirit Lake were even more profound. From just four miles away, Mount St. Helens had unleashed a hot blast of gases, ash, and rock debris into the lake—almost immediately after the massive avalanche—raising the lake's level and damming its outlet. The following pyroclastic flows pouring into the lake raised the temperature of the water to almost 100 degrees F.; no life could have survived.

Spirit Lake went through the same drastic chemical changes that the smaller lakes did, but on such a large scale that there were doubts the lake could ever support life again. But in just five years the recovery of the water chemistry was almost complete. Besides the action of beneficial bacteria that helped clear the lake, heavy rains and melting snow added copious amounts of fresh water, and the action of wind and waves added oxygen. Aquatic insects, frogs, and plants started to appear and

New vegetation on the Pumice Plain seen from Johnston Ridge. PHOTO ©KIRKENDALL-SPRING

rainbow trout—apparently released by an impatient fisherman—flourished.

By 2005, many of the floating logs had sunk, though mats of them still move across the lake when the wind blows. One unexpected consequence: the lake—which used to freeze over every winter—has not frozen since the eruption. Scientists believe that with the surrounding forest gone, the lake is no longer protected from winter winds that blow across the lake, moving the floating mats of logs around: thus "stirring" the water and preventing ice from forming.

The most surprising development was discovered in 2005, when a limnologist measuring the clarity of the water found it was the clearest it had been since measurements were first taken in 1937. Spirit Lake today, though shallower than before the 1980 eruption, contains the same volume of water and its surface elevation is 240 feet higher than prior to the eruption.

If you want more detailed information about the many facets of the recovery process, look for a new book "Ecological Responses to the 1980 Eruption of Mount St. Helens" published in 2005, with twenty chapters written by the scientists who for many years have conducted this groundbreaking research.

Researcher with grasses from Spirit Lake, 2006. PHOTO ©ROGER WERTH

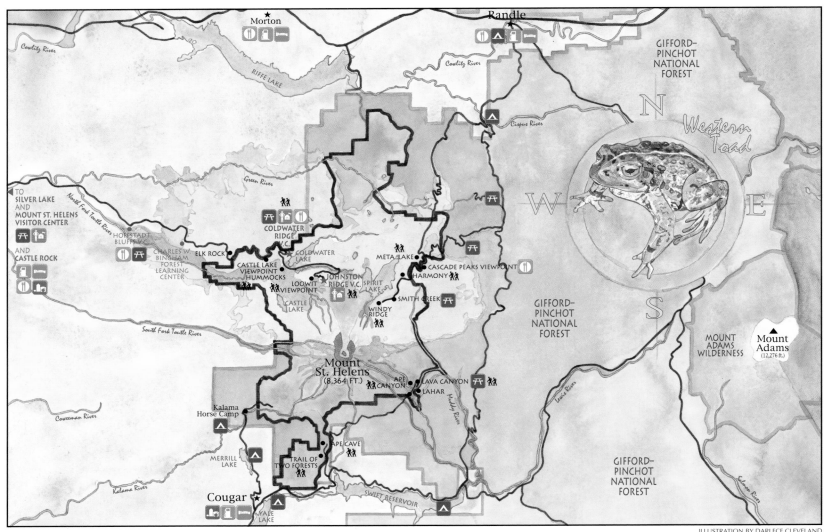

ILLUSTRATION BY DARLECE CLEVELAND

Just a few days after the May 18th eruption, the U.S. Forest Service and the U.S. Geological Survey had an important visitor. President Jimmy Carter had flown to Mount St. Helens to see for himself the volcanic devastation that had occurred. He toured the command center in Vancouver, Washington, and then was taken on a helicopter tour led by two forest service officials and a group of geologists that included my husband Bob. A scientist at heart, the President asked penetrating questions about the warning signs, the eruption itself, and its aftermath. He also indicated how important it would be to have the area preserved as a national park or monument.

Achieving that goal was not simple; the land holdings on and around Mount St. Helens were a checkerboard pattern, with the USFS in charge of about half, but the rest held by various logging companies and the State of Washington.

Oddly enough, the section of land containing the volcano's summit was owned by Burlington Northern Railroad. The USFS was eventually able to acquire that parcel through land exchange—an agreement the railroad was probably glad to make.

After a series of creative land agreements was completed, the new national monument was created. On August 27, 1982, then–President Ronald Reagan signed a law setting aside 110,000 acres around the volcano as Mount St. Helens National Volcanic Monument. It was one of the first national monuments to be managed by the U.S. Forest Service rather than the National Park Service.

With thousands of people from all over the world flocking to Mount St. Helens to see this phenomenon of nature, it was evident that there would have to be tight restrictions to protect visitors from volcanic hazards. It was also evident that the volcano would need protection from an over-

enthusiastic public.

Outside the monument the damaged forests are being logged and replanted. Inside the boundaries, the entire 110,000 acres have been set aside to study Nature's intricate process of healing itself. Trail use is controlled to keep hikers from wandering through carefully planned research areas.

The stated purpose of the monument is to encourage research, education, and recreation. To meet those goals a new paved road—the Spirit Lake Memorial Highway—was constructed to replace the old highway that was destroyed by the avalanche and mudflows, and three state-of-the-art visitor centers have been built.

**ABOVE:** Steam rising from early dome in Mount St. Helens' crater, September 1984.
PHOTO ©JEFF GNASS

**PAGE 44/45:** Field of lupine and Douglas-fir at Lahar. PHOTO ©JACK DYKINGA

Scientist on rockfall from dome, June 2006.
USGS PHOTO by JIM VALLANCE

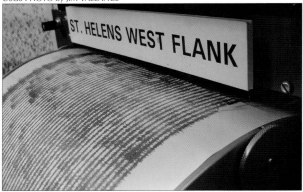

Seismic drum at Johnston Ridge Observatory, October 2004.
USGS PHOTO by JOHN CLEMENS

Ice-encased remote camera at the "Sugarbowl" location.
USGS PHOTO by STEVE SCHILLING

Preparing the Silver Fox Drone for flight.
USGS PHOTO by JOHN PALLISTER

Soon after Mount St. Helens stirred to life in March 1980, scientists from the U.S. Geological Survey and universities across the country started to converge on Vancouver, Washington. Their mission was twofold: to learn as much as possible about the mysterious inner workings of volcanoes and—for the USGS—to provide state and local authorities with reliable warnings of volcanic hazards.

The USGS established an Emergency Coordination Center at the Vancouver office of Gifford Pinchot National Forest, inevitably bringing crowded and hectic conditions to a previously well-organized office—obviously not a permanent solution. After the major eruption of May 18, sporadic volcanic activity continued throughout the summer, and many scientists pressed for the establishment of a permanent observatory at Mount St. Helens. Others felt that setting up a permanent observatory was premature—that activity could suddenly stop and the stream of valuable data that was pouring in would dry up. But by late 1980, the decision had been made by the Washington office to establish the David A. Johnston Cascades Volcano Observatory (CVO), in memory of the young geologist who was killed in the eruption.

The scope was broadened to include monitoring of the Cascade Range in Washington, Oregon, and California. It was formally dedicated in 1982, a sister facility to the Hawaiian Volcano Observatory, which had been established in 1912 and had pioneered most of the methods of monitoring volcanoes used around the world. Since then the USGS has added Alaska Volcano Observatory, Long Valley Observatory (California) and Yellowstone Volcano Observatory.

As the CVO mission statement explains, "Observatory scientists, technicians, and support staff work in partnership with colleagues at other USGS centers, universities, and other agencies to:

1. Monitor restless volcanoes and provide timely warnings of eruptions,

2. Assess hazards from volcanoes, including water-related hazards in valleys draining volcanoes,

3. Share volcano information with emergency-management and planning officials,

4. Develop new techniques and methods to better monitor and predict behavior of volcanoes,

5. Study volcanic processes, and

6. Educate public officials, citizens, and the news media about what volcanoes can do."

CVO is also headquarters for a rapid response team of volcanologists called the Volcano Disaster Assistance Program, or VDAP. Team members are ready to respond to threatening volcanic activity anywhere in the United States or in other parts of the world, carrying with them portable monitoring equipment and many years of personal, hands-on experience with active volcanoes.

## TOOLS OF THE TRADE

When a dormant volcano is stirring itself awake—whether from a long sleep or a short nap—the first signs usually come from seismic signals. This was true at Mount St. Helens in March 1980, when seismographs at the University of Washington recorded a swarm of small earthquakes under the mountain. Continuing micro–earthquakes raised the alarm that something ominous was happening.

In monitoring volcanoes, the two most useful tools for geologists are earthquake studies and deformation measurements. Earthquake studies provide vital information for determining the eruptive state of a volcano. Networks of seismic stations continuously monitor Mount St. Helens and many other Cascade volcanoes. Data are gathered from recording instruments and analyzed by computers. A particular type of seismic signal, known as a harmonic tremor, seems to indicate that magma is moving underground and an eruption may be imminent.

Deformation studies involve careful and precise measurements of changes in the volcano's surface dimensions before, during, and after eruptions. A volcano typically swells with magma before an eruption and deflates afterwards. Cascades Volcano Observatory uses sophisticated instruments to measure changes in the total amount of uplift or downdrop, and minor changes in horizontal distances.

When Mount St. Helens erupted in 1980, the main tool available for studying deformation was the Electronic Distance Measurement (EDM), which used a geodimeter, a laser-beam device, to measure distances with great precision.

In the years since 1980, EDM techniques have been almost completely replaced by the use of the Global Positioning System (GPS), which uses satellites and portable or fixed receivers to determine the relative positions of ground surface stations. Radio code and time signals broadcast by the satellites arrive at the survey stations and are compared by computer analysis. Elevations and distances between two receivers can be measured with an extraordinary degree of accuracy.

Many other monitoring techniques are being employed—and refined—at CVO, including the tiltmeter, which works on the principle of a giant carpenter's level to measure the "tilt" of a volcano's surface. Studies in gas geochemistry are also valuable. The Correlation Spectrometer (COSPEC) was the standard for detecting sulphur dioxide ($SO_2$) for decades, but recent technological improvements have resulted in a much smaller, cheaper, and more advanced instrument, the Differential Optical Absorption Spectrometer (DOAS) for accomplishing the same goal. Gravity and magnetic studies are also proving to be important tools. With a computerized system, most data can be compared automatically on a common time base.

Probably the most innovative and versatile device in use at Mount St. Helens is the "spider"—a stainless-steel frame about six feet tall that carries an array of sensitive instruments. It can be lowered by helicopter onto the dome or glacier to do a variety of tasks. Powered by batteries, each spider holds a GPS receiver that gives three-dimensional readings showing movement or growth of the dome or glacier. It also has a sensor to measure changes in gas emissions, which could show movement of magma beneath the surface. There is also a seismometer, which is attached to the spider but is mounted separately to minimize wind vibrations, and a microphone to record sound waves. A computer on the spider reads the sensors, then logs and sends the data to the observatory through the radio. Spiders operate in dangerous territory; several have been damaged or destroyed by dome explosions or rockfalls.

Setting up GPS equipment on the crater rim, September 2004.
USGS PHOTO by MIKE LISOWSKI

Preparing "spiders" for placement in the crater, November 2004.
Uncredited USGS PHOTO

Analyzing gasses with a Correlation Spectrometer, October 1983.
USGS PHOTO by LYN TOPINKA

Researchers setting up "tiltmeter" in the crater, August 2005.
USGS PHOTO by DAN DZURISIN

# THE REAWAKENING

Crater eruption, October 1, 2004. USGS PHOTO by JOHN PALLISTER

In the summer of 2004, the staffs of both Mount St. Helens National Volcanic Monument and Cascades Volcano Observatory started making plans to commemorate an important date—May 18, 2005—the twenty-fifth anniversary of the 1980 eruption of Mount St. Helens. But then, right on cue, as if not wanting to sleep through her own party, Mount St. Helens started to stir again.

During the last week of September 2004, swarms of small earthquakes beneath the volcano caught the attention of scientists. Each day the quakes increased both in frequency and intensity, with patterns that were eerily similar to those of March and April 1980 preceding the eruption. A few of the volcanologists currently at CVO had been studying Mount St. Helens ever since the major eruption. University of Washington graduate student Elliot Endo, who first suspected that those quakes of early 1980 were related to volcanism, was now, twenty-five years later, Scientist-in-Charge at CVO.

Backlit steam plume, November 4, 2004.
USGS PHOTO by JIM VALLANCE and MATT LOGAN

Earthquake activity steadily increased until October 1, when a huge plume of steam and ash jetted two miles into the sky. Large rocks were tossed around the crater and a vent was blown through the crater's glacier. The activity delighted crowds of onlookers, including a group of sixteen geology students who were at Johnston Ridge on a field trip.

Scientists hurried to replace instruments that had been destroyed in the October 1 explosion. They deployed more seismometers, for a total of eight, and briefly entered the crater to attach a GPS instrument to a new dome that had started growing between the old dome and the crater wall. A lava dome grows from magma pushing up from below; more dangerous than it looks, it is a brittle shell of cooling lava capping an explosive mix of gas and molten rock.

Eruption plume Mount Adams, March 8, 2005.
PHOTO ©BRUCE ELY/THE OREGONIAN

The new dome was an unusual shape often called a "whaleback," after it was described by a reporter as "looking like a whale shouldering its way to the surface." It continued to grow vigorously in the following months. By February 2005, it had grown to 1600 feet in length, was 500 feet wide, and was 530 feet higher than the old 1986 dome. There was visible uplift of the crater floor, and the dome was expanding so rapidly it cracked the glacier almost in half.

Ironically, the glacier had just been given a name by the Washington State Board of Geographic Names—*Tulutson*, the Cowlitz Indian word for ice. Scientists had been studying the glacier with great interest since it started to form in the late 1980s. It has been growing on the inside of the south wall of the crater from accumu-

Aerial view of steam plume and crater, sunset, April 26, 2005.
USGS PHOTO by JOHN PALLISTER

**OPPOSITE:** Mount Rainier, Spirit Lake, and the dome in Mount St. Helens glowing at sunset, September 2005. PHOTO ©TYSON FISHER

Eruption plume seen from CVO Offices, Portland, Oregon, March 8, 2005.
USGS PHOTO by MATT LOGAN

lating snow that becomes so heavy it compresses into ice and remains shaded by the crater wall for much of the year. It has been of special interest because it is so rare for scientists to be able to see a glacier grow from scratch. There have been fears that it would be blown apart or melted by volcanic heat and cause flooding, but as of this writing—in late 2006—*Tulutson* is somewhat warped but surviving.

Intermittent bursts of activity have continued since the October 2004 events, with a spectacular outburst on the afternoon of March 8, 2005. A team of USGS scientists was in a helicopter near the volcano at the time and watched ash and steam boil upward, reaching 15,000 feet in minutes, and then continuing to rise to 36,000 feet. Clearly visible from Portland, Oregon, it generated much interest and drew more spectators to the mountain. Geologists speculated that the new dome had been blown apart, but when they could get a close look they found it largely intact. Volcanic gases or steam explosions likely fed the blast, spewing from cracks or vents that were later obscured by falling ash and rocks.

Activity has continued through 2006, with a massive new "fin"—a 300-foot-tall spine of lava sprouting from the new lava dome. Rockfalls and small emissions of steam and ash are still common.

The question is always asked, "What will Mount St. Helens do next?" and the answer is always "No one knows for sure." One likely scenario is that the dome will keep growing episodically over many years, eventually filling the crater and going on to build a new peak similar to the old one. Or a sudden explosion like those in the mid-1980s could blow the dome apart and building would start over. Or the dome growth could stop and the volcano might stay silent for many years. Whatever happens will probably have an element of surprise. As one volcanologist has said, "Mount St. Helens hasn't yet done all the dances she knows."

Researcher viewing crater with "spine", August 25, 2006. USGS PHOTO by JULIE GRISWOLD

Helicopter collecting rock samples from the "spine," April 28, 2006. USGS PHOTO by DAN DZURISIN

## AERIAL VIEWS OF THE "WHALEBACK"

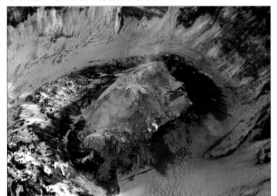

Birth of the "whaleback," November 7, 2004.
USGS PHOTO by JOHN PALLISTER

November 29, 2004.
USGS PHOTO by JIM VALLANCE and MATT LOGAN

February 22, 2005.
USGS PHOTO BY STEVE SCHILLING

Shattered "whaleback," April 10, 2005.
USGS PHOTO by JON MAJOR

## VIEWS FROM CRATER RIM CAMERA

June 29, 2006.
USGS PHOTO

July 15, 2006.
USGS PHOTO

August 3, 2006.
USGS PHOTO

August 27, 2006.
USGS PHOTO

## VIEWS FROM BRUTUS CAMERA

November 29, 2004.
USGS PHOTO by DAN DZURISIN

February 22, 2005.
USGS PHOTO by DAN DZURISIN

July 26, 2005.
USGS PHOTO by STEVE SCHILLING and HELENA BUURMAN

July 26, 2006.
USGS PHOTO

**PAGE 52/53:** The eruption of March 8, 2005, seen from Castle Lake Viewpoint. PHOTO ©TYSON FISHER

# VISITING THE MONUMENT

A visit to Mount St. Helens National Volcanic Monument is an opportunity to see the two faces of Nature: its incredible destructive power, and, even more impressive, the tenacity with which life—in its many forms—survives and renews itself.

The monument is accessible by roads from the west, the northeast, and the south, each with very different features. Driving distances are long, so if you only have one day for a visit your best choice would be the trip up Spirit Lake Memorial Highway (Washington Highway 504) for the most varied experience. This is a handsome, 52-mile road that was built after the major eruption and follows the North Fork of the Toutle River, ending with the overwhelming views from Johnston Ridge. However, from this side you won't have a view of Spirit Lake or the extensive blowdown zone.

If you are visiting any time except mid-summer, some monument roads and visitor centers may be closed. You can check for information with Monument Head-quarters (360-449-7800). You may also want to call to check on weather conditions, to ensure good volcano viewing. Spirit Lake Highway is paved and open all year as far as Coldwater Ridge, but many roads on the northeast and south sides are routinely closed in winter. Coldwater Ridge Visitor Center is open much of the year, but Johnston Ridge Observatory is closed in winter. The state-run Mount St. Helens Visitor Center at Silver Lake—at the bottom of Spirit Lake Highway, just off Interstate 5—is open all year for limited hours, and is a good place to inquire about visibility and weather conditions at the Coldwater and Johnston Ridge facilities.

There are no overnight accommodations inside the monument, so plan to lodge in one of the neighboring towns. Except for backcountry camping, there is no camping within the monument's boundaries, but there are forest service, state, and private campgrounds on all sides of the monument. The most convenient camping is at Seaquest State Park, just across the road from Silver Lake Visitor Center.

Inside monument boundaries, the only food service is at Coldwater Ridge Visitor Center, so take a picnic or plan to stop for lunch before or after you see the monument. Also, there are no gas stations in the monument so be sure to start each day with a full tank.

There are many good hiking trails in the monument, ranging from short interpretive trails near the visitor centers, to backcountry access, to the strenuous climb to the summit of Mount St. Helens. Be sure to check at the nearest visitor center for trail conditions, and for permits where needed. Access to the summit and to some backcountry trails may be restricted if there are any signs of volcanic activity in the crater.

Johnston Ridge Observatory. PHOTO ©KIRKENDALL-SPRING

Hikers on crater rim with Mount Adams visible above the clouds. PHOTO ©BRUCE ELY/THE OREGONIAN

Coldwater Ridge Visitor Center. PHOTO ©TERRY DONNELLY

**OPPOSITE:** Mount Hood seen through standing dead trees near Smith Creek Viewpoint. PHOTO ©LARRY ULRICH

## THE WEST SIDE

If you have just one day to visit Mount St. Helens National Volcanic Monument, your best choice is the western approach to the park on Washington Highway 504, otherwise known as Spirit Lake Highway. This route has not only the most varied and spectacular scenery but it has five informative visitor centers along the way, each with a different focus.

Before 1980, this was the road to the recreation areas at Spirit Lake and the mountain, but it was almost totally destroyed by the avalanche and mudflows that coursed down the Toutle River in the hours after the eruption. The highway was rebuilt in the early 1990s. It doesn't go to Spirit Lake anymore, but ends at Johnston Ridge Observatory.

Mount St. Helens Visitor Center at Silver Lake is a good orientation stop. This handsome building next to a wetlands area was built by the U.S. Forest Service but is now managed by the Washington State Parks Commission. The actual boundary of the national monument is still thirty-five miles ahead, but at this visitor center you will find informative exhibits focusing primarily on the human story of the monument, audio-visual presentations, and, on a clear day, a grand view of Mount St. Helens across Silver Lake.

Beyond Silver Lake, the road follows the North Fork of the Toutle River. For mile after mile you see evidence of the massive mudflows that coursed through here on May 18, 1980. In some places the flows reached twenty to thirty feet above the normal river level. None of the original bridges were left standing; all were rebuilt when the new road was realigned and rebuilt, to stay higher on the canyon's slopes in anticipation of the next eruption.

Hoffstadt Bluffs Visitor Center, owned by Cowlitz County, is another good stop for visitor information. A short trail starting near the visitor center leads to Memorial Grove, planted in honor of the fifty-seven people who were killed in the 1980 eruption. All the names of this diverse group are listed on a plaque in the grove. There are dramatic views from here down into the Toutle River Valley, with still-evident avalanche and mudflow deposits. Hoffstadt Bluffs Visitor Center has meal service, a gift shop, and in the summer and early fall, helicopter tours of the area are available from an office near the parking lot.

The trees just past Hoffstadt Bluffs were in the "Scorch Zone," where they were killed but not blown down by the huge blast from the volcano. Beyond here is the "Blowdown Zone," where all the trees were felled by the eruption blast. In both zones the trees were intensively logged and the areas replanted. In some places, the layer of volcanic ash was so thick and compacted that augers were used to drill holes down into the underlying soil so that new seedlings could be planted.

On the private lands outside monument boundaries, foresters started replanting trees just a month after the eruption. Over the next seven years, 18.5 million new trees were planted—almost all fast growing Douglas-fir. The replanted forests you see along the road now have a different appearance from the original forests here since they are not the naturally occurring mix of conifers and hardwoods. In January 2005, the lumber companies started thinning and harvesting the first stands of trees that were planted twenty-five years earlier; the rest will be harvested in about another fifteen years.

Steaming, 90-degree water of Toutle River, May 19, 1980.
PHOTO ©ROGER WERTH

New bridge at Hoffstadt Creek, April 1998.
USGS PHOTO by ED KLIMASAUSKAS

Replanted hillsides outside the monument along Spirit Lake Highway. PHOTO ©JEFF D. NICHOLAS

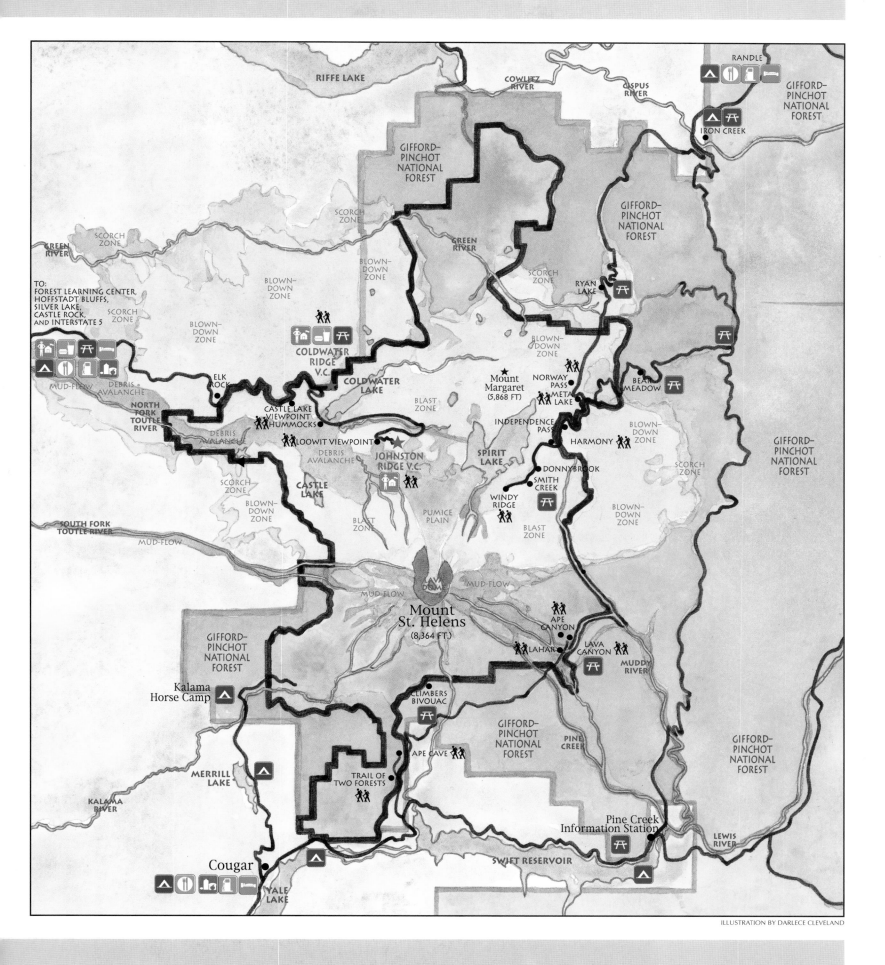

ILLUSTRATION BY DARLECE CLEVELAND

Early morning at Coldwater Lake, created by the debris avalanche of May 18, 1980. PHOTO ©JEFF D. NICHOLAS

Mount St. Helens seen from The Hummocks Loop Trail, 2004. PHOTO ©JEFFREY L. TORRETTA

New vegetation and the Pumice Plain seen from Johnston Ridge, 2004. PHOTO ©JOHN MARSHALL

A few miles up the road, at Milepost 35, The Forest Learning Center uses effective displays to explain forest management. It tells how the forest environment was affected by the eruption, emphasizing salvage, recovery, and reforestation. This visitor center is a collaboration among Weyerhauser Company, Washington State Department of Transportation, and Rocky Mountain Elk Foundation. On a small hill by the parking area, the Rocky Mountain Elk Foundation has installed telescopes that afford grand views of the Toutle River Valley and, with luck, the sight of a herd of returning Roosevelt elk, which like to browse on the lush new vegetation in the valley.

Coldwater Ridge Visitor Center is a major stop, both for visitor information and impressive views. From Coldwater Ridge you have a closer view into Mount St. Helens' crater, seven miles away.

This visitor center focuses mostly on the environmental recovery at the monument. Exhibits vividly show Nature's two faces—the overwhelming destructive power of natural forces, and the tenacious resilience of life. Take the short (one-third mile) Winds of Change interpretive trail near the visitor center and see for yourself the intricate interactions of Nature. Coldwater Ridge Visitor Center has meal service and a well-stocked bookshop.

Beyond Coldwater Ridge Visitor Center, Coldwater Lake is worth a stop. This lake did not exist prior to the 1980 eruption; it was created when the debris avalanche from Mount St. Helens dammed the valley of South Coldwater Creek. Take the short (one-half mile) Birth of a Lake Trail, a barrier-free loop along the shore. Interpretive signs along the way explain the formation of the lake after the 1980 eruption. Some of the hummocks left by the avalanche protrude as islands from the west end of the lake.

For a closer look at the intriguing hummocks—some more than 100 feet tall— stop at the trailhead just past the Coldwater Lake turnoff and walk all or part of the 2.5-mile Hummocks Loop Trail. In addition to the colorful hummocks, the trail passes ponds and marshes—all part of the terrain created by the debris avalanche. This is a good place to look for elk, especially in the spring.

Loowit Viewpoint—a few more miles along Highway 504 on Johnston Ridge— affords a breathtaking view into Mount St. Helens' crater. A romanticized version of an Indian legend tells of the mountain as a witch (Loowit) who could transform herself from beauty to beast and back to beauty again—as the volcano has done several times in its history.

At the end of the highway—at milepost 52—is Johnston Ridge Observatory, named for geologist David A. Johnston who was killed near here when the hot volcanic blast swept his observation post away. This is a working observatory, monitoring the seismic activity beneath Mount St. Helens, but it also has many fine interactive scientific exhibits vividly depicting the explosion and avalanche. Be sure to watch the stirring film that recreates the cataclysmic events of May 18. The most memorable part of a trip to Johnston Ridge is the unsurpassed view into the heart of the steaming crater, just 5.5 miles away. Its growing lava dome seems like a living presence.

## THE NORTHEAST SIDE

A trip to the northeast side of Mount St. Helens National Volcanic Monument provides some unforgettable views of volcano country—and stark evidence of the power of the volcano's lateral blast, still vivid after twenty-six years. At least as impressive are the signs of life returning to the countryside—carpets of wildflowers at Bear Meadow, small trees growing and thriving, and all forms of wildlife returning in numbers greater than anyone expected.

From Highway 12, at the town of Randle, turn south on Highway 25 and then right on Road 99. Stop at the Bear Meadow parking area, and try to imagine what it must have been like to stand here on the morning of May 18—11.5 miles from Mount St. Helens—and see a huge eruption cloud surging toward you.

Two photographers—Gary Rosenquist and Keith Ronnholm—were among the group camped here, hoping for a great view of volcanic action. They took remarkable photographs of the start of the eruption, and barely escaped with their lives when the cloud engulfed them. A series of photos taken by Rosenquist were not only visually stunning but proved invaluable to volcanologists, who were able to study in detail the sequence of the eruption.

As the ground-hugging cloud kept advancing—topping ridge after ridge—the photographers and other campers ran for their cars and started down the road. Lightning bolts shot between portions of the cloud and ash the consistency of mud rained down. Lighter ash followed, almost completely obscuring visibility, but after a trip that took hours, all the campers miraculously made it to safety.

Ghost forest along Road 99 near Ghost Lake, 1999.
PHOTO ©FRED HIRSCHMANN

A couple of miles past Bear Meadow is the beginning of the blast zone. Trees here were killed but left standing when an explosion cloud, estimated to exceed 500 degrees in temperature, surged through here. A few miles farther along the road from here and you enter the blowdown zone, where all the magnificent old-growth forest was toppled by the blast. Dense, black, ground-hugging clouds of steam and rocks swept over four major ridges and valleys, reaching as far as seventeen miles to the west, and 10.5 miles to the east, from their source. Wind speeds reached a maximum of several hundred miles per hour.

The trees here have been left just as they fell, allowing scientists studying this area to piece together the swirling patterns within the fast-moving blast cloud. Closer to the crater, old-growth trees of some six feet in diameter were uprooted and blown away, while farther away the trees were all blown down.

Stop at Meta Lake and take the short (one-half mile round trip) barrier-free paved trail to the lake's shore. Meta Lake was in the blast zone, only 8.5 miles from the crater. A large, mature forest that surrounded the lake was destroyed, but the lake itself was protected by a thick blanket of ice and snow when the eruption happened.

Mount St. Helens seen from Bear Meadow, July 2000.
PHOTO ©JEFFREY L. TORRETTA

The trees you see around the lake now are silver fir, which were small enough to be completely covered by the protective banks of snow. Now out from under the shade of the older trees, they are growing rapidly. Trout, salamanders, and frogs as well as insect larva somehow survived, even though the lake was choked with ash and debris as the ice melted. Beavers also soon returned. They have built dams that have raised the lake level somewhat.  As a reviving ecosystem, Meta Lake is a success story.

About four miles after leaving Meta Lake, stop at Harmony Viewpoint for a grand view of Spirit Lake.  If you have time for a short hike, a steep trail (2.2 miles round trip) leads to the lakeshore—the only public access to Spirit Lake. A rustic resort, Harmony Falls Lodge, used to sit on the lakeshore just to the west of the end of the trail. The lodge site—now under almost two hundred feet of water—was accessible only by boat and is remembered fondly as a tranquil retreat.

Spirit Lake seen from Donnybrook Viewpoint.
PHOTO ©GEORGE WUERTHNER

Mount St. Helens and Spirit Lake seen from near Norway Pass.
PHOTO ©JEFF GNASS

The blasted landscape near Windy Ridge.
PHOTO ©PAT O'HARA

The lush forest along the Trail of Two Forests.
PHOTO ©JEFF D. NICHOLAS

From Windy Ridge, at the end of the road, is one of the most breathtaking views you will find at Mount St. Helens. Here, at 4,000 feet in elevation, the mountain is four miles away; you can see the volcano's 8,364-foot summit, the top of the new dome within the jagged horseshoe-shaped crater, and Spirit Lake below at an elevation of 3,446 feet.

Take time to read the informational signs. They point out other important landmarks such as Pumice Plain, the avalanche deposits, Elk Rock, Johnston Ridge, Harry's Ridge, and Mount Margaret.

The huge avalanche that triggered the May 18th eruption swept down from Mount St. Helens into the lake and ran more than eight hundred feet up the ridges on the other side. The blast followed almost immediately and then the hot pyroclastic flow surged across the avalanche deposits. Although the avalanche started first, the velocity of the lateral blast was so much greater that it overtook the avalanche before it reached the far side of Spirit Lake. The blast shattered and uprooted the trees there, and they in turn were carried back into the lake by the backwash of the water that had been displaced, covering the surface with floating logs. Many of the logs have disappeared by now—some sink every year—but many are still visible in the "bathtub ring" high on the shore.

So much material had plunged into the lake—not just avalanche debris but tons of organic matter from trees, plants, and animal carcasses followed by tons of falling ash—that it was feared the lake could never recover and support life. Nature again held a surprise; after only five years—thanks to the action of beneficial bacteria and huge amounts of fresh water from rain and melting snow, plus the action of wind and waves stirring the lake—the chemistry of the water was almost back to normal. Spirit Lake now supports a variety of plant and animal life that has returned to its waters. The lake is shallower now, but with a larger surface area it contains the same amount of water as the original lake.

At the north edge of the Windy Ridge parking lot, a short (one-quarter mile), steep trail—called the Sand Ladder—leads to a hilltop with a great view of Spirit Lake and a look across into the gaping crater with its growing lava dome.

## THE SOUTH SIDE

If you have already spent some time sightseeing on the north and east sides of Mount St. Helens, you have witnessed scenes of almost unimaginable destruction, traveling mile after mile through ruined forests. The images are still vivid, even after more than twenty-five years. After that experience, a visit to the south side of the monument will seem to be like turning back the clock. Since the major blast on May 18, 1980 was directed principally toward the north, except for some mudflows, the south side almost completely escaped the devastation. Several sites here, though, offer intriguing glimpses into Mount St. Helens' volcanic history.

About ten miles past the town of Cougar, take a walk on the fascinating Trail of Two Forests. Almost 2,000 years ago, a series of very fluid basaltic lava flows—the type of lava common in Hawaii but very unusual on Cascade volcanoes—poured down this side of Mount St. Helens. It killed and buried a mature forest of large trees, mostly conifers. The few trees that were left standing burned away but left pits called tree molds; in many of them you can still see impressions of patterns of the trees' bark. Other trees that were knocked down and buried by the flows slowly burned away under the hardening lava, leaving cavelike horizontal tree molds. At one point along this quarter-mile trail, it is possible to climb down a ladder into one of the vertical molds and then crawl for about fifty feet through one of the horizontal tree molds (if you really want to!).

A new forest is now growing on top of the flow with trees, ferns, and mosses building a new life on top of the destroyed forest. Interpretive signs explain how a sequence of plants can eventually grow and thrive on a once-forbidding lava flow. A boardwalk trail winds through the forest, protecting the fragile new growth while providing easy walking.

Just beyond the Trail of Two Forests is Ape Cave, another type of volcanic feature known as a lava tube. Ape Cave formed in one of the same fast-moving lava flows that coursed down here almost 2,000 years ago. A lava tube is formed when the outer crust of a lava stream cools and solidifies, but the molten interior continues to flow. After that interior flow has drained away, a long hollow tube is left behind.

More than 13,000 feet in length, Ape Cave is one of the longest lava tubes in the continental United States. Discovered in 1951, it was eventually explored—and named— several years later by a group of Boy Scouts who called themselves "The Mount St. Helens Apes."

A hole broken in the lava tube's roof (called a skylight in volcano country) provides an entrance into the cave; the lower cave extends 4,000 feet downslope, and the upper cave extends more than 7,000 feet upslope. The walk through the lower cave is relatively easy, though it requires sturdy shoes and, since the temperature is about 42 degrees, a sweater is a good idea. There is no light in the cave, so it is essential to carry a good flashlight or lantern and extra backup batteries (available for rent near the cave's opening during the season.) The upper cave requires a strenuous scramble over broken rock piles, best left to serious cavers.

Lahar Viewpoint, near the end of road 83, is one of the few sites on the south side of Mount St. Helens where some of the effects of the May 18th eruption can be seen. *Lahar* is an Indonesian word meaning volcanic mudflow; lahars are especially destructive in Indonesia, where many active volcanoes are surrounded by densely populated farming villages. Here you can see the wide, barren deposit where a flood of mud, water, and rocks swept down Pine Creek that day in 1980. It's easy to imagine how devastating such a flow would be to a mountain village.

About a mile past Lahar Viewpoint is Lava Canyon, an old valley that was filled by ancient lava flows. The upper Muddy River has cut a channel through the canyon, exposing intriguing layers of old flows. Some of the May 18th mudflows—flowing down a pre-existing channel—also coursed through here, exposing and ripping away older deposits and creating new channels for cascades and waterfalls. The first half-mile of the trail is barrier free for wheelchair access.

The climbing route to the summit of Mount St. Helens is also accessed from the south side, from the Climber's Bivouac at 3,750 feet in elevation. While not a long climb it is an arduous trip, for experienced climbers only, but the views from the 8,364-foot summit are unmatched. To look down into the jagged, gaping crater with its still-growing lava dome is unforgettable, but to see towering Mounts Rainier, Adams, and Hood in the background is a reminder of what Mount St. Helens once was and may once again be—centuries in the future.

The climbing route may be closed if the volcano exhibits any unusual activity. In any case, climbing permits are required for the trip, and are available online.

South side of Mount St. Helens reflected in pond near Lahar.
PHOTO ©FRED HIRSCHMANN

Rubble and layered ridge exposed by mudflows at Lahar.
PHOTO ©JEFF D. NICHOLAS

Waterfall on the Muddy River, Lava Canyon.
PHOTO ©JEFF D. NICHOLAS

**ABOVE:** Mount St. Helens and Spirit Lake seen from the Mount Margaret backcountry, sunset. PHOTO ©TYSON FISHER

## IN CASE OF EMERGENCY

**Emergency & Medical**
Call 911

## FOR MORE INFORMATION

**Mount St. Helens**
**National Volcanic Monument**
  Monument Headquarters
  42218 NE Yale Bridge Road
  Amboy, WA 98601
  (360) 449-7800
  www.fs.fed.us/gpnf/mshnvm
  —or—
**Mount St. Helens Visitor Center**
  3029 Spirit Lake Highway
  Castle Rock, WA 98611
  (360) 274-0962
**Northwest Interpretive Association**
  3029 Spirit Lake Highway
  Castle Rock, WA 98611
  (360) 274-2125
  www.nwpubliclands.com
**Hoffstadt Bluffs Visitor Center**
  Milepost 27, Highway 504
  (360) 274-7750
  www.mt-st-helens.com
**Forest Learning Center**
  Milepost 33, Highway 504
  (360) 414-3439
  www.wy.com/sthelens
**USGS Cascades Volcano Observatory**
  1300 SE Cardinal Court
  Building 10, Suite 100
  Vancouver, WA 98683
  http://vulcan.wr.usgs.gov

## LODGING INSIDE THE MONUMENT

There is no lodging avaliable within the Monument.

## LODGING OUTSIDE THE MONUMENT

**Cowlitz County Visitor Services**
  1900 7th Avenue
  Longview, WA 98632
  (360) 577-3137
  www.co.cowlitz.wa.us/tourism

## CAMPING INSIDE THE MONUMENT

There is no camping permitted within the Monument.

## OTHER REGIONAL SITES

**Fort Vancouver National Historic Site**
  612 E. Reserve Street
  Vancouver, WA 98661
  (360) 696-7655x10
  www.nps.gov/fova

**Mount Rainier National Park**
  Tahoma Woods, Star Route
  Ashford, WA 98304
  E-mail: MORAInfo@nps.gov
  (360) 569-2211
  (360) 569-2177 (TDD)
  www.nps.gov/mora

**North Cascades National Park**
  810 State Route 20
  Sedro-Woolley, WA 98284
  (360) 856-5700
  www.nps.gov/noca
**Olympic National Park**
  600 East Park Avenue
  Port Angeles, WA 98362
  (360) 565-3130

www.nps.gov/olym

## NATIONAL FOREST INFORMATION

**Columbia River Gorge**
**National Scenic Area**
  902 Wasco Street, Suite 200
  Hood River, OR 97031
  (541) 386-2333
  www.fs.fed.us/r6/columbia/forest
  www.fs.fed.us/r6/colville
**Gifford Pinchot National Forest**
  10600 NE 51st Circle
  Vancouver, WA 98682
  (360) 891-5000
  www.fs.fed.us/gpnf

**Mount Hood National Forest**
  16400 Champion Way
  Sandy, OR 97055
  (503) 668-1700
  www.fs.fed.us/r6/mthood

## SUGGESTED READING

Carson, Rob. MOUNT ST. HELENS. Seattle, WA; Sasquatch Books, 2000.

Dale, Virginia, Frederick Swanson and Charles Crisafulli, Eds. ECOLOGICAL RESPONSES TO THE 1980 ERUPTION OF MOUNT ST. HELENS. New York, NY; Springer, 2005.

Decker, Robert and Barbara Decker, MOUNT ST. HELENS NATIONAL VOLCANIC MONUMENT. Mariposa, CA; Sierra Press, 1997.

Decker, Robert and Barbara Decker. VOLCANOES IN AMERICA'S NATIONAL PARKS. Hong Kong; Odyssey Guides, 2001.

Decker, Robert and Barbara Decker. ROAD GUIDE TO MOUNT ST. HELENS. Mariposa, CA; Double Decker Press, 2002.

Harris, Stephen, FIRE MOUNTAINS OF THE WEST. Missoula, MT; Mountain Press Publishing Co., 1988.

Hickson, Catherine. MOUNT ST. HELENS: SURVIVING THE STONE WIND. Vancouver, BC; Tricouni Press, 2005.

Hill, Richard. VOLCANOES OF THE CASCADES: THEIR RISE AND THEIR RISKS. Guildford, CT; The Globe Pequot Press, 2004.

Northwest Interpretive Association. MOUNT ST. HELENS NATIONAL VOLCANIC MONUMENT TRAIL GUIDE. Seattle, WA; Northwest Interpretive Association.

Quiring, Jim. MOUNT ST HELENS: THE CONTINUING STORY. Las Vegas, NV; KC Publications, 1991.

Thompson, Dick. VOLCANO COWBOYS: THE ROCKY EVOLUTION OF A DANGEROUS SCIENCE. New York, NY; Thomas Dunne Books, 2000.

Waitt, Richard. EYEWITNESS CHRONICLES: CATACLYSMIC ERUPTION OF MOUNT ST. HELENS. Washington State University Press, 2007.

**ABOVE:** Aerial view of the "whaleback" in Mount St. Helens' crater and Mount Hood, 2005.
PHOTO ©BRUCE ELY/THE OREGONIAN

## PRODUCTION CREDITS

Publisher: Jeff D. Nicholas
Author: Barbara Decker
Editor: Nicky Leach
Illustrations: Darlece Cleveland
Printing Coordination: Sung In Printing America

ISBN 10: 1-58071-069-7 (Paper)
ISBN 13: 987-1-58071-072-5 (Paper)
©2007 Panorama International Productions, Inc.

Sierra Press is an imprint of Panorama International Productions, Inc. All rights reserved. No part of this book may be reproduced in any form without written permission from the publisher. Printed in the Republic of South Korea.
First printing, Spring 2007.
Second printing, Spring 2009.

### SIERRA PRESS

4988 Gold Leaf Drive, Mariposa, CA 95338
(209) 966-5071, 966-5073 (Fax)

VISIT OUR WEBSITE AT:
**www.NationalParksUSA.com**

**OPPOSITE**
Sunrise view from the crater rim with Spirit Lake and Mount Rainier, 2005. PHOTO ©TYSON FISHER
**BELOW**
Spine emerging from the dome in Mount St. Helens crater, 2006. PHOTO ©STEVE NEHL/THE OREGONIAN